SPACE

to process

S P A C E

to process

a conversation: stories and journaling prompts for parents of children with disabilities

SARAH M. SPEAR

Cover design by Marilyn Murray
Author's photograph courtesy of Belmont University

ISBN 979-8-9927599-0-7 (paperback)
(also available as an e-book)

Publisher's Note
While the author has made every effort to provide accurate information and references at the time of publication, the author does not assume any responsibility for errors or for changes that occur after publication. Further, the author does not have any control over and does not assume any responsibility for referenced resources or their content.

This is a work of creative nonfiction. All of the events in this collection are true to the best of the author's memory. The views expressed in this collection are solely those of the author.

Contents

About This Book

Journaling has been a lifelong practice for me. When I'm worked up about an incident, I sit down and write out my thoughts. I take a look at my perspective and wonder why I feel and think that way. I explore the same situation from the perspectives of others involved. The mere practice of committing all those thoughts to paper clears them from my head and creates space for peace.

This book is organized as a type of conversation between us. Imagine you and I sitting down to chat about life's ups and downs. After you listen to my story, you'll be prompted to respond with your own story. In so doing, we're creating space to process what we've gone through. I also share my experiences to assure you that you're not alone in your struggles. You'll find resources in the Appendix that have helped me and may prompt further responses from you.

Since we're starting up a conversation, I'll tell you a little about myself. My daughter, Miriam, is eleven years old and lives with Wiedemann-Steiner Syndrome, a rare genetic disease that is accompanied by many co-diagnoses including autism. My son, William, is eight years old and does not live with any identified diagnoses. In true disability advocate fashion, my daughter loves to say, "nothing about me without me." Way to go, Miriam! This has sparked many conversations between the two of us about her story being hers to tell and my story being mine to tell. Being Miriam's mom and caregiver is central to my story. In this book, I endeavor to tell my story without crossing the line into telling her story, or my son's story, for that matter. Where is that line? Well, that's its own story and journaling prompt (see page 66)! Perhaps you can relate to that tension. I've attempted to share with you my experiences as a caregiver while also retaining my family members' autonomy to share their experiences when and how they would like.

In my years of working in disability advocacy, so many impactful connections have come from sharing my perspective as the mom of a child living with a disability. You might also be in the mom category, but if you're a dad, a grandparent, a foster parent, a guardian, or someone who cares in another capacity for a person living with a disability, I hope you will still find the reflections and prompts useful. Take a look at the table of contents if you're in the mood to reflect on something specific.

After each story, I include questions that my experiences prompted me to reflect on. When other questions come to you, follow those. We receive the greatest benefit by exploring the questions on our own hearts. Most importantly, have fun with this and give yourself grace! When big emotions come up, take time to sort through those, perhaps with a trusted friend. If you need to set this book aside for awhile, go right ahead! This is YOUR space to process.

Your Unique Approach to Parenting

John and I were living in St. Louis when we hosted some friends from India. We all planned to go out for dinner but I felt so nauseous I couldn't join in. As I sat in bed, eating chicken noodle soup and crackers, I started to wonder if I could be pregnant. Sure enough, that was it! My husband, John, was three months away from an Air Force deployment to Afghanistan. The timing wasn't ideal but we had planned on having kids, so it was go time!

A LOT of stuff happened over the next nine months (John's deployment, my brother's death, getting forced out of my job, my daughter's birth, and moving cross-country), so I hardly knew which way was up. Miriam came into the world and we hit the ground running. I never really paused to consider *how* I wanted to care for Miriam. I just took the next step immediately in front of me.

This section is intended to slow you down, carving out time for you to define your unique approach to parenting. You'll write about the values, boundaries, and provider mindsets that are important to you as you make caregiving decisions.

Values That Guide Us

In my home, I regularly hear the phrase, "nothing about me without me." Miriam usually says this when she realizes I've been making decisions she wants to be a part of. Especially as she gets older, she should expect to have a say about the things that impact her. For example, Miriam has been taking ballet lessons and overcame significant anxiety to perform in the Christmas show. Once she made it through that, she decided she didn't want to take ballet lessons anymore. She'll finish up the semester then try something new. One of my parenting values is including my kids, to the extent possible, in decision making that affects them.

What values shape the way you make decisions about caring for those you love?

Boundaries That Uphold Our Values

In my family, we strive to have dinner together multiple times each week. Over the course of dinner, each family member shares what happened that day. Sometimes we'll reflect on current affairs and upcoming events. This is also a time when we share our hardships and encourage one another. Life can be tough; family dinner is our response to life's challenges. We make a conscious effort to only participate in one or two evening activities, per person, each week in order to preserve this time. This includes my husband and I, too.

What aspects of your family's lifestyle are most important to you? What boundaries help you uphold those norms?

The Kinds of Providers We Want

I sat in Miriam's doctor's office, watching her doctor talk with her. In this medical practice, the physician completes the entire visit, from taking vitals to discussing concerns and administering vaccines. I had mentioned that Miriam previously had difficulty having her blood pressure taken so the doctor lowered the lights and spoke in soothing tones. Sure enough, once the cuff tightened, Miriam started panicking and wriggled off the table. The doctor remained calm, continued to speak in soothing tones, and continued with the rest of the exam, acting as though a near-meltdown was no big deal! This calm approach is part of the mindset I look for in Miriam's providers.

What are your ideal providers' ways of thinking, doing business, and habits?

Receiving a Diagnosis

My phone lit up and I recognized the geneticist's phone number. "Hello," I answered.

"Hi, Sarah, it's Dr. So-and-So. We got the results back from Miriam's whole exome sequencing. They're consistent with a rare disease called Wiedemann-Steiner Syndrome (WSS). We'll be sending you the results in the mail but I wanted to call to let you know."

"Wow, OK, thank you. What else can you tell me," I asked.

"Well, it's a rare disease and there's a Facebook group for parents that you might find helpful. There really isn't anything more for our office to do at this point, although you're always welcome to schedule another appointment if it would be helpful," the doctor responded.

And thus, after six years of searching, Miriam's developmental delay had a name and an explanation. Our previous visits to geneticists and developmental pediatricians included a chromosomal microarray to identify any genetic variations. Our search had been taking place since Miriam was born and we finally had her diagnosis.

Miriam had already been diagnosed with ADHD, a diagnosis that commonly coexists with WSS, and she would later be diagnosed with anxiety and autism, also common among people with WSS. I think of WSS as the umbrella diagnosis that all her other diagnoses fall under. The one genetic variation that causes WSS also helps modify the expression of other genes. This creates a snowball effect that impacts all realms of Miriam's life.

I've learned that my family's lengthy, circuitous journey to receive a rare disease diagnosis is more the norm than the exception. From the numerous medical visits to the doctor's call relaying the diagnosis, our experiences were par for the course. My prevailing feeling upon hearing the diagnosis was relief. The more I read about WSS, the more relief I felt because everything I read helped me make sense of who Miriam is. WSS helped me conceptualize what's going on inside her and causing things like her extra long eyelashes and behavioral challenges.

What was your journey to your child's diagnosis like? How did you initially feel when you received a diagnosis? How did your feelings change in the early days following the diagnosis? This is such a big question for many of us that you've got some extra space to process.

Did I Cause This?

I was sitting on a therapist's couch, trying to get a handle on my tumultuous interactions with my daughter, when the therapist asked if I'd heard of the refrigerator mother theory. The now debunked theory says that a lack of maternal warmth causes autism in children. My therapist noted how I experienced a lot of trauma throughout my pregnancy, delivery, and postpartum period. She surmised I did the best I could, given the circumstances, but Miriam had formed an insecure attachment with me.

I left that session angry and dubious. I had never before wondered, "did I cause this?" Now, I couldn't press pause on that refrain. Was I so cold and unfeeling in the wake of my brother's death that I failed to attend to Miriam's needs?

This was long before we had a diagnosis for Miriam. Now I can see what a gift that diagnosis was. It freed both my husband and me from the burden of believing we had caused our daughter's rare genetic disease that was literally encoded in every cell in her body. Her diagnosis gave us language to explain that the disease sometimes manifests in meltdowns and other behaviors that challenge our capabilities as parents.

But before I knew all that, I wrestled with doubt and blame, wondering if I caused Miriam's hardships. In retrospect, I could have also asked if I caused her effervescence and high sociability, if I caused her creativity and spontaneity. Since I was asking if I caused the hard parts, why wasn't I asking if I caused the stellar parts, too? We're usually harder on ourselves than others, though, and this burden of blame is something many parents struggle with.

What hard moments in your life does this story bring to mind? How have you worked through the hard feelings?

When Grief Hits

As I work with parents, I hear a common refrain that is worth our consideration: grief. This feeling might emerge when a parent first receives their child's diagnosis. Sometimes they're confronting the loss of their dreams for their child and their family. Sometimes grief comes as their fears are confirmed. Closely linked to grief is denial. Perhaps my kid will be the one to best the averages, to upend the projections. Hey, anything's possible *and* there's value in grappling with likely outcomes.

I remember being on my hands and knees in the hallway, drying up water that my daughter had thrown during a meltdown. My son was cowering in his room, frightened by his sister's behavior. My husband was doing his best to contain our daughter. I started crying, thinking, "this is my life now. This isn't how I imagined it would be for any of us in this family." Of course, that moment wasn't the end of our story, but when grief hits, it hits hard.

When has grief overcome you? What triggered your response? If you could go back to that hard moment, what would you tell yourself?

Dealing with Holiday Stress

It was mid-December. As the song "It's the Most Wonderful Time of the Year" played, I asked myself, "is it really?" Don't get me wrong. As a Christian, I get excited to celebrate Christ's birth, yet my family is not immune to the additional stressors that accompany this season. There's just MORE – more special events, more shopping, more excitement, more anxiety. There's also LESS – less structure, less predictability, less free time, less calm. Just reading those sentences begins to induce stress! If you're with me, pause to take a few deep breaths to calm your body.

The shift came when my kids hit toddlerhood. I would feel the impending holidays coming at me like a tsunami. My inner monologue went something like this: "They're coming, I can't escape, hopefully I can hang onto something to anchor me so I don't get washed away." I've instituted some practices to keep me grounded (see Appendix) and I've also recognized this is a good time of year for me to pause and reflect. What's happening now that is within my control and what's not?

Think about your current or most recent holiday season. What were things you dreaded doing and did anyway? Some things that come to mind are staying up late to watch the ball drop and getting family portraits. Write about what caused you to respond as you did. How did you feel about what you ended up doing?

Healthy Boundaries

Generally, school is a place where my daughter has a lot of structure and always knows what's expected of her. However, mid-December of last year, the trifecta of more sugar, less sleep, and loss of structure hit. I arrived at school to help in my son's classroom and was met, instead, by a shaking, shivering daughter, walking down the hall towards me in distress. She had a panic attack for the first time in school and the anxious behaviors we had been observing at home spilled over to school. Those behaviors stuck around after her panic attack and were generalized to all environments. This catalyzed a months-long reaction that impacted our whole family and extended family, too. Winter break last year was far different from what we had expected.

This experience helped me clarify where we needed to create boundaries. For example, we created a new boundary of staying in our home for Christmas so we have the tools and familiarity to navigate whatever challenges arise.

How about you? What boundaries have you put in place or would you like to put in place to preserve the health of your family members?

What Our Tears Tell Us

My middle school teacher wisely said that tears wash the windows of our souls. Sometimes those windows get dirty and we need tears to wipe them clean and renew our perspective. The things that make me cry give insight into who I am and what's going on in my life at a deeper level.

Recently, I watched my daughter's first ballet performance. I cried when a complete stranger came up to me at intermission and told me I'm doing a great job parenting. I cried during the performance, thinking of all my daughter had to overcome to be up on that stage. I cried when text appeared above the stage, saying that God's unfailing love cannot be shaken. Those tears all pointed to intentional love. That's the kind of love that doesn't always come easily, when both being loved and loving are choices we make before we feel it. There's a lot of choosing love as the parent of a child with my daughter's specific disability. My tears reminded me to persevere and continue receiving and giving love.

What's the last thing that made you cry? Why? What does that reveal about what's moving in your heart these days?

Disability and Faith

I grew up in a Christian home and I grew up surrounded by disability. Once I became a parent caring for a child with a disability, I began exploring the interplay of faith and disability. Exploring might be too polite. I experienced an outright reckoning. I had questions that needed answers beyond what I'd received. I had to reconcile a world where people lived with disabilities with an ableist church culture and with a God who healed, but not always. I was dissatisfied (and sometimes angry) with explanations of disability resulting from sin entering the world. People living with disabilities are created in the image of God. How might their disabilities reflect God's image?

This single issue has probably propelled me further in my faith journey than any other issue. It has caused me to seek out sages and scrutinize scripture. It has caused me to make hard decisions about church. I have not arrived at an answer, but I'm grateful for how the questions have shaped me spiritually.

How has your experience with disability shaped you spiritually? What questions have you grappled with and where have you experienced joy on your own spiritual journey?

Control in Decision Making

Over the years, I've gained a sense of what Miriam enjoys and the kind of instruction and activity she thrives under. I've steered her towards activities I thought would be a good fit, ones with plenty of supports that have accommodated participants with disabilities in the past. As we prepared for this school year, I braced myself when Miriam said she wanted to play flute in her school band, take ballet lessons, and do intramural sports. Combined with all the other new things this year, including a new school and new support team, I wasn't so sure about these new activities. "You've always enjoyed being in Chorus," I said, thinking that would be so much easier than flute. "Ballet has lots of rules," I intoned.

There we were – two people with two very different ideas of what would be enjoyable and tolerable for my daughter. It was tempting to wrest control of the situation, making an executive decision about what Miriam would and would not participate in. This was a perfect example, though, of Miriam's favorite saying, "nothing about me without me." Miriam ended up trying all the new things. Some activities worked out better than others, but the point is that she was in control of deciding for herself.

This reminds me of the concept of Dignity of Risk. People living with disabilities are often denied opportunities by their caregivers to take risks, a dignity that ought to be available to all people. If I'm being honest with myself, much of my hesitation in Miriam trying these new activities came from fearing the risk that she'd fail or find the activities frustrating or end up with unsympathetic instructors. But none of my fears signaled the end of the world. Relinquishing control in this situation resulted in Miriam getting to decide for herself what she wanted to do and what an appropriate level of risk was. Those are self-determination skills I want her to cultivate, that will serve her well as an adult.

When have you experienced a situation like this? How did you go about making a decision?

Dealing with Our Anger

As water flooded the kitchen floor, I stared in horror, wondering what I was thinking. I no longer recall what triggered my anger but my daughter and I had gotten into a vicious cycle of dysregulation during that season. The cycle would begin with some transition, such as leaving the house, then my husband or I would deny a last minute request from Miriam, and then she would begin melting down. We would remain firm and she would become violent. I would start yelling and so would she. Things continued spiraling downwards from there.

This particular day, we were preparing to go on a hike. I had a CamelBak water bladder in my hands, filled with 2½ liters of water, when I reached my breaking point. In my anger, I slammed the water bladder to the ground, it popped open, and water went everywhere. I was working with a therapist who encouraged me to recognize when my anger got to 6 on a 10 point scale. The therapist said that no good would come after I got to a 7, so I had to do whatever it took *before then* to calm down and regulate myself. I'd gotten way beyond a 7 at the point I flooded our kitchen.

In the intervening years, I've acquired skills to better regulate my emotions. It started with me literally locking myself in my room when I was reaching my breaking point so I wouldn't be a hazard to those around me. I'm better able to remain calm and help my daughter co-regulate but that progress came over time and sometimes isn't obvious.

Does this sound familiar? What does dysregulation look like in your home? How are you learning to manage big emotions, both yours and your child's?

Struggles of Siblings

I snuggled with my six year old son, William, after a particularly rough bedtime routine. While his sister was having a meltdown, he alternated between hiding and animatedly jumping around. His response reminded me of when I hold my hands over my eyes during the scary parts of a movie. Part of me wants to see what happens, and part of me doesn't. This was Will as he witnessed the emotional and physical whirlwind unfolding in our home.

While Will loves telling stories, he gets really quiet when I bring up emotions. I started asking him yes/no questions, instead. "Does it feel scary when that happens?" He nodded. "Are you afraid of what might happen to Dad and me?" He nodded. "Do you feel like you need to be well behaved to make up for your sister's hard time?" He nodded.

My heart broke a little. THIS is what I wish so many of my friends and family members could understand. A little boy was bearing the weight of the world on his tiny shoulders. I assured him that Mom and Dad know what to do and that we are not in danger in those situations. I assured him that he is free to be himself — Dad and I understand he's a kid who will make mistakes and that's OK. I tried to communicate, in concepts that a six year old would understand, that he's not responsible for his sister's behavior and he doesn't need to compensate for it.

How do the siblings of your child who lives with a disability respond to meltdowns and hard times? Has that changed over time? How has your response to the siblings also changed over time?

Special Times with Siblings

One month, I resolved to have a date with each member of my family. My son eagerly anticipated our date. I asked him if he wanted me to tell him what was planned or to keep it a surprise. It remained a surprise until we pulled up to Fork and Band, a slingshot shooting gallery. What boy wouldn't love that kind of adventure?

Well, about 15 minutes in, we hit turbulent waters. My son, Will, was missing the targets and wasn't interested in any coaching from me or the staff. He told me, "this isn't fun, it's horrible!" We sort of redeemed the experience with pancakes at a diner but he was already dreaming up exactly what he wanted for our next date.

In early January we set out again, hot chocolates in hand, to realize his dream date of looking at Christmas lights. I had researched a neighborhood that was widely known for their displays. We parked, got out, and began walking through the winter wonderland. I saw a faint glimmer of a smile as my decoration-loving son admired all the lights. He estimated there were 1,000 different decorations which inspired him to dream of how he wanted to decorate our house next year.

What are ways that your neurotypical kids like to be engaged by you? What have you learned about them that surprised you? What traditions do you have together?

To Medicate or Not to Medicate?

When Miriam was in elementary school, her teachers noticed difficulty in her ability to attend to the task at hand. We were observing the same at home. For example, Miriam was able to pick out clothes and dress herself if my husband or I stayed with her to encourage her to complete the task. Most activities of daily living were similar.

Miriam had already been diagnosed with ADHD so it was natural for us to discuss medication options with her developmental pediatrician. The doctor was well-versed in working with and prescribing medications for children with ADHD. My husband and I were the reticent ones. We didn't want to seek a prescription to merely make our lives easier, as if we couldn't cope with our own child. We also wondered if we had done our due diligence in considering dietary, physical activity, and therapeutic supports. Looking back now, that reticence seems silly but we've all got to go through our own process in coming to terms with medication intervention.

We had to trial a couple stimulants to find one Miriam tolerated well. Once we found the one, the difference was appreciable. Instead of losing her personality or becoming a zombie, Miriam was still warm and engaging and also able to attend to the task at hand. We noticed a difference at home and her teachers noticed a difference at school.

Fast forward a couple years and, once again, Miriam was having difficulty attending to tasks. Evaluations completed by teachers and parents confirmed a medication adjustment was in order. We increased Miriam's stimulant. Within days, Miriam became more aggressive. We witnessed levels of lashing out that we hadn't seen in a long time. In the absence of any other appreciable changes to the routine, we narrowed our focus on the medication. Ultimately, Miriam discontinued that medication. Any benefit of her increased ability to attend wasn't worth the increased aggression.

Since then, Miriam's medication journey has continued with additional ups and downs. What has that journey been like for you? How have you felt about introducing medications? Has that shifted? If so, how?

When Peers Don't Care

Standing beside the school bus, I heard the bus driver tell kids to, "move over!" For the third week in a row, Miriam's peers were not making space for her to sit down on the bus. Their excuses ranged from, "I need a seat to myself," to, "we're in the middle of a conversation and don't want to move." We live in a small town so I know these kids; they're not "bad" kids. Despite all the reasons I know I shouldn't get worked up, my Mama Bear instinct comes out and I just want my kid's humanity to be acknowledged.

We all encounter these kinds of situations. Perhaps we appeal to the authority (I called the principal about the bus), perhaps we coach our kids on standing up for themselves, perhaps we sigh and hope it won't happen again. Miriam could ride the short bus but that's not the point, is it? I want Miriam to ride the bus *she* wants to ride; I want her peers to willingly scoot over if she needs a seat. I want society to recognize the inherent dignity that our kids possess. My heart breaks when that's not the case.

When has your child encountered this kind of interaction with their peers? What internal conflicts did this bring up for you and how have you sorted through those?

Mental Health Crises

Though Miriam had experienced some short-lived panic attacks with our immediate family, a couple years ago she experienced a true mental health crisis that destabilized her for months. At first, I thought we just had to get through a stressful season and then we'd return to our steady-state. Instead, as a family, we had to gear up for an extended season of grace and encouragement as we faced this together. The limits of our patience and kindness were tested and, I'd like to think, expanded. John and I had to persevere in modeling peace in the face of repetitive, anxious behaviors. Miriam's younger brother had to grow in overlooking the behaviors that got under his skin. Miriam got a chance to grow in self-advocacy as she explained to our extended family what was going on.

That time was scary. Immediate solutions were lacking and I didn't know when or if things would return to what we were used to. Turns out, we were able to return to less anxiety through medical interventions but that took time, patience, and wisdom. Have you been through this kind of season? Perhaps you're right in the thick of it. What triggers you and tests your limits? How do you cultivate peace when feeling surrounded by wreckage?

Finding Friends

"Let's get together over summer break," Miriam's classmate effused on the last day of school. Numbers were exchanged and soon after I got a text, asking if Miriam could use the phone. They made plans to meet up.

That summer was beautiful – filled with laughter, dancing, and joy. Miriam invited her friend to some of her favorite places. Her friend shared her musical creations. They had disagreements and they persevered in figuring things out. They both intentionally reached out to the other and kept in touch. It was the first time I can recall Miriam having a mutual friendship wherein each child valued the other for who they are.

Friendships can be tough for our kids. How has your child's experience with friends been similar and different? What do you hope for your child when it comes to friends?

Inclusion in Community Activities

Following Miriam's foray into ballet, she decided to try gymnastics. I stopped by a local studio to ask about classes and chatted with the owner. I let the studio owner know that Miriam has a rare genetic disease that affects how she learns and asked if the owner thought their classes would be a good fit for Miriam. While getting Miriam registered, the studio owner sent me this message: "Can you let me know again what to tell Miriam's teachers on the best way to help her learn in the gym?"

That small question filled me with hope. Not only was the studio owner welcoming of Miriam but she also wanted to set up Miriam and her instructors for success. I no longer take that kind of intentionality for granted. It can be challenging to make space for neurodivergent kids who learn differently. For example, Miriam learns by repetition and by copying her peers. This requires coaches to repeat information and physically place Miriam in places where she can see her classmates. As a staunch advocate for meaningful inclusion, I believe neurodivergent kids have a right to take up space wherever they are. I try to navigate the tension between taking up space and receiving necessary supports by dreaming of a truly inclusive world while, at the same time, taking steps for my daughter to be included in the here and now.

How do you honor this tension of both/and, knowing your kid deserves to take up space and knowing they sometimes benefit from support to take up that space?

When Other Parents Just Don't Get It

You know those times when you've got to say something uncomfortable to another parent and you really don't want to? After months of putting it off, I finally got up the gumption to reach out to another mom about how her child was excluding Miriam. We regularly saw this family and our kids all interacted with each other. After I described the interactions I'd witnessed, the mom said that I had misunderstood the situation and the way I characterized her child was inaccurate.

This scenario has replayed itself numerous times with numerous parents. I try to explain to the parent what's going on and seek a cooperative solution. I try to embody the same kind of humility I hope I'd demonstrate if our roles were reversed. I'm often stonewalled. In the immediate aftermath, I'm usually angry, then I become bitter and want to check out, and then I consider what grace in this situation looks like. I'm left examining how I handled the situation and where to go from here.

The reality is that we can only control our own actions and responses. I wish I could force kids to be nice. I wish I could get other parents to recognize that even their kids are capable of behaving unkindly, but I only get to control how I approach these situations. When I'm on the receiving end, I can remain humble and engage my kids in conversations about how they're treating other kids. When I'm providing feedback, I can do it in a timely manner. I can remain rooted in the facts and gracious in the conversation.

What's this like for you? When have you wrestled with what is and is not within your control? How do you determine whether and how to engage in difficult conversations with other parents?

What We Love About Our Kids

At bedtime, my kids open up and we have the most heartfelt conversations. One night, Miriam was curious about why I was shutting down my startup. She sat up, a mournful look on her face, and gave me a big hug. She remarked that it must be hard for me and wondered what I was going to do. I was able to share with her about my startup journey and how I was processing this loss. What impressed me that evening was how precious, loving, and kind Miriam is. I lose sight of this in the day-to-day so I'm grateful when her compassion breaks through, encouraging me.

During a particularly difficult season of parenting, a therapist suggested I create artwork capturing what I appreciate about Miriam. The therapist also suggested I keep the art somewhere I would regularly see it. Years later, that artwork remains inside my closet door. (My son has noticed it and wondered why it's there.) There are so many admirable qualities about my daughter I can overlook during difficult seasons. I'm grateful for when her finer qualities come through and communicate her love for those around her.

When have you been pleasantly surprised by your child's response to a situation? What character qualities did they reveal? What other aspects of their personality do you appreciate?

Expertise v. Energy Exercise

When I was building my last company, I participated in a program where we had to take stock of all the activities we did for our companies over the course of three months. Some of those tasks were daily and some were only quarterly. The point was for us to get a list of all the things we had to do over a quarter. Next, we plotted our ongoing activities across a matrix of Personal Expertise versus Energy Required to complete the activities.

I've used a similar concept when working with groups of parents. First, we take stock of all the parenting-related activities we undertake over the course of a three-month period. Then, using the matrix included on the next page, we plot out each of these activities.

We'll start with the first part and then we'll consider how to interpret your matrix.

List below all the ongoing tasks you engage in as a caregiver.

Expertise v. Energy Matrix

Using the matrix below, plot your ongoing activities according to how skilled you are at each activity and how energizing each activity is for you.

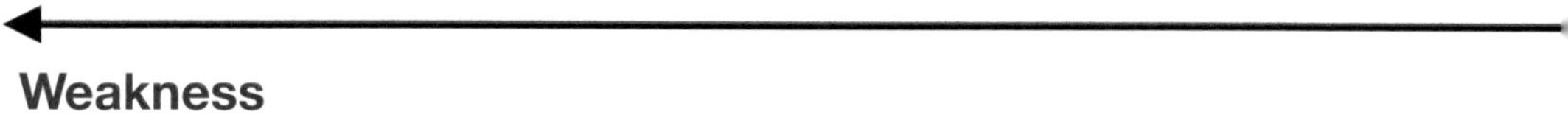

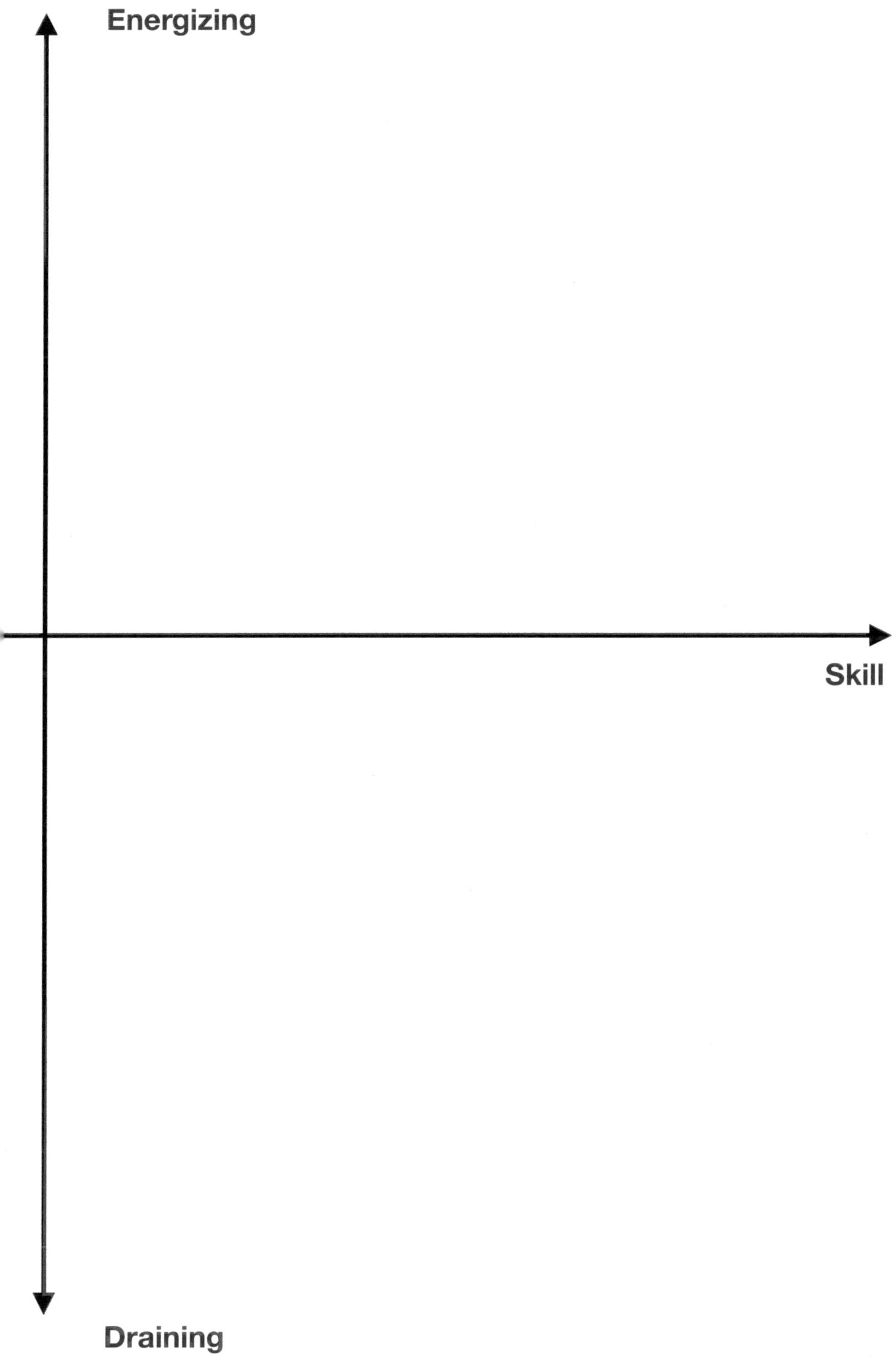
Energizing
Skill
Draining

Expertise v. Energy Debrief

Every so often, I return to this Expertise v. Energy Exercise. What I'm looking for are ways to optimize the activities that have to get done. As we move through the quadrants, focus on just two or three of your plotted activities when answering the questions.

Let's start with the upper right quadrant. These are activities that energize you and that you're good at. How could you spend more of your time in the Strength/Energizing quadrant, perhaps leaning into two or three tasks in this quadrant?

Expertise v. Energy Debrief, cont.

Moving to the upper left quadrant, these are activities that energize you, though you're not great at them (yet). What would it take to strengthen your skills required for two or three activities in the Weakness/Energizing quadrant?

Expertise v. Energy Debrief, cont.

In the lower left quadrant, you plotted activities that drain you and require skills you're weak in. How could you spend less of your time in the Weakness/Draining quadrant? Are there two or three activities where you could get additional help? This might mean leaning on a family member or friend. Maybe your child's school could provide support here.

Expertise v. Energy Debrief, cont.

Finishing up in the lower right quadrant, you're strong at the skills required for these activities but they drain you. For what two or three activities in the Strength/Draining quadrant could you remain the expert, but oversee someone/something who does most of the work? Maybe there's an app that could complete the activity (e.g, executive functioning app) or a local high schooler you could hire to help out.

Holding Down a Job

I sat in my home office, reviewing a project for the nonprofit where I worked. I heard the garage door go up, the Jeep pull in, the sound of feet running up the stairs, and the office doorknob turn. Before I knew it, I was in the middle of a flurry of hugs and tears and exclamations. I needed just 30 more minutes to finish work but the kids needed me to resolve a conflict right then and there.

This is but one example of the ongoing tension of being a parent and an employee. Working for myself makes it a little easier since I set my own deadlines and can work around doctors' appointments, but it's still a juggling act. Work travel exacerbates the challenges. It's nice to get away but there's a LOT of planning that goes into being away, figuring out whether and how often I'll call home, and then re-entry. Life as a working parent is inherently challenging. Adding disability to the mix makes it even more so.

Where do you experience similar tension between your various responsibilities? What rhythms have helped ease the tension? How has this changed as your child has gotten older?

Finding Our People

Sitting by a hotel pool, I chatted with a mom I'd just met as our kids splashed around. We instantly dove into the proverbial deep end … What kind of medication does your daughter take? What kind of school does she attend? How about friends? … The conversation ranged from bodily functions to celebrations. Miriam and I were attending the Wiedemann-Steiner Syndrome (WSS) Foundation's International Family Conference where we met this family from the UK. Our girls just clicked – we'd found our people.

That entire weekend, we were surrounded by families that "got it," no explanations required. When a girl was melting down because the craft teachers didn't have time to guide her through the craft, we jumped in to ask for the materials so we could do the craft with the girl. When a young man was having a hard time in one of the sessions on sibling interactions, a mom jumped up to MC so the man's mom could take a break outside with him. We learned about discussing consent with our kids and the latest research on the WSS mouse. The kids danced and laughed together.

WSS is a rare genetic disease that is characterized by a developmental delay, intellectual disability, unique physical characteristics, and behavioral dysregulation. Meltdowns are the norm, not the exception. Many individuals living with WSS use G-tubes and require frequent surgeries. School and friends are generally tough. Being in a room with 70 families that all experience this reality is a gift.

Describe how it feels when you find people who just get it, no explanations required. If it's been hard to find that, what's your dream for what it would be like?

Decisions About School

When Miriam was in preschool, she hadn't received her Wiedemann-Steiner Syndrome diagnosis yet. We were operating with the understanding that she had a global developmental delay. When Miriam was finishing her second year of preschool, John and I were carefully weighing whether a third year of preschool might be beneficial for her. During Miriam's Planning and Placement Team (PPT) meeting, we asked what the school's expectations for kindergarteners were. The principal jumped in to say, "Miriam has an Individualized Education Program (IEP) so she'll get whatever accommodations she needs in kindergarten."

After the meeting, one of Miriam's PPT members called me to encourage John and I to advocate for a third year of preschool. They said that Miriam was on the young side compared to her peers and an extra year to develop would benefit her, likely for the rest of her schooling.

While the details of each kids' IEP differ, the idea of a parent advocating for their child probably resonates with you. Though parents are members of the PPT, it can feel overwhelming to be the only non-school member in a conference room with 10+ professionals. When have you encountered push back on what you thought was best for your child? What did you learn in navigating that situation?

The People with Big Dreams for Our Kids

Before a PPT meeting, Miriam's Social Worker said he was looking forward to seeing what and who Miriam would become. His comment caught me off guard. I assumed that he would be skeptical of what Miriam could reasonably accomplish. I was early in my parenting journey and didn't want to get my hopes up; I wanted to remain realistic. His words, though, stuck with me and gave me hope when I needed it. What an encouragement it was to hear a professional who'd spent plenty of time interacting with and observing Miriam say that he envisioned her living independently. He encouraged me to dream of the possibilities.

I still don't know what Miriam's future holds. What I do know is that there have been people along the road, like Miriam's Social Worker, who've held up a candle in the darkness. These folks have served as lamp posts along the way, reminding me to maintain hope and buoying my spirits when they've flagged.

Who's someone who served this purpose in your life, offering you hope right when you needed it? What was the situation and how did their presence shift your perspective?

Who Bears the Responsibility for Inclusion?

Recently, I facilitated a support group for caregivers. During our time of sharing what was hard, a mom expressed frustration over her neurodivergent son's situation. He was being penalized for failing to conform to neurotypical norms of behavior. His neurotypical peers, however, were able to navigate the social system and faced no penalty. I've felt similarly about Miriam's interactions. She struggles to pick up on social cues. She feels the weight of trying to conform to social standards. Her peers don't bear the same burden of making space for neurodiverse ways of being.

I'm still waiting for the inclusion groundswell to include neurodiversity. For example, the Americans with Disabilities Act (ADA) of 1990 legislates that businesses, as places of public accommodation, comply with accessibility standards as outlined in the law. These standards largely encompass accommodations for mobility, Deaf/Hard of Hearing, and Visual disabilities. Business owners legally bear no responsibility for making their businesses accommodating to neurodivergent customers. The responsibility for finding neurodiverse-friendly businesses falls to the neurodivergent customer. I've met many business owners who had never considered how to be more inclusive of neurodivergent customers. Our conversations got them thinking and possibly changing their business practices as a result.

What do you think? Who bears the responsibility for including neurodivergent people in society? Broadening the question, who bears responsibility for including people with disabilities and/or rare diseases in society? What have you seen in practice and what do you hope the future will be like?

Whose Story Is It to Share?

I had the chance to share my family's story with a class of students who were studying everything from Speech and Language Therapy to Psychology. As I was preparing my slideshow, I used some of Miriam's artwork for the backgrounds. These works of art provided insights into how Miriam's mind worked. They also provided a helpful chronology of events as I shared our story.

My preparation was going swimmingly until Miriam discovered what I was doing. Immediately, she got angry and asked what I was doing with her artwork. She fumed, "nothing about me without me!" What was I to do? I quickly agreed that I should have talked about this with her beforehand because sharing our family's story was certainly about her. I also explained that I was asked to share our story so that students could learn from us.

I didn't navigate that situation perfectly. I'd already agreed to speak so I fulfilled my commitment. Miriam was still upset and still felt left out of my decision making process. But don't worry – I've had plenty of chances to practice since then. Maybe your child gets upset about you talking about them or maybe they could care less. Either way, how do you determine what's yours to share and what's theirs to share? Where's the line? Further, what circumstances dictate what you share? How does that vary, depending upon whom you're talking with, how long it's been since the situation occurred, etc?

Transition to Adulthood

Miriam loves found object art known as assemblage. She collects glitter and fragments of paper as she goes through her day, turning it all into spectacular collages. Recognizing Miriam's proclivity, a family member gave Miriam a book featuring various careers in art. This book was a great prompt for talking with Miriam about her interests. It'll be something we return to as we continue that conversation.

Miriam and I recently started talking about the transition program in our school district. Students living with disabilities can participate until they're 22. Most of the students are learning life skills and getting job training. Miriam and her Planning and Placement Team will hopefully do person-centered planning over the next few years to determine what she wants to pursue and how she'll do that.

How have you approached your child's transition to adulthood? Depending upon your child's age, what do/did you anticipate being important considerations for what your child does after high school?

Beyond Childhood

Parents whose kids are older than mine have blessed me with the gifts of friendship and sharing their experiences. These wise souls model patience, humor, and tenacity with a good dose of realism thrown in. One time, a mom friend was attending an out-of-town wedding with her family, including her 40 year old Autistic daughter. I said, "I hope it's a good time," to which she responded, "Oh, it'll be a time, whether good or otherwise!" These parents keep it real.

Another time, a mom lamented that she couldn't find any occupational therapists willing to work on feeding with her 27 year old daughter. I was in the business of tracking down resources for families but I drew a blank on finding a professional who could meet this need. Parenting an adult child who lives with a disability can be tough. You know better than anyone that it's not all roses. You've probably heard more times than you can count that you and your child inspire others. People reflect, "I don't know how you do it," or perhaps, "I couldn't do what you're doing." You might've thought, "of course you could do it, and you would if you found yourself in my position!"

Thinking back to the Parenting Perspective this journal began with, how has your perspective on parenting shifted as your child has aged?

Checking In

As we come to the end of our time together, conversing about our memories and hopes for the future, I want to take a moment to check in. How are you? Has it been one of those days/weeks/months/years? I wish I was there to give you a big hug and encourage you by listening to your story, marveling at how you've persevered. Perhaps you're rocking life right now and you're in a good place. Woohoo! Getting there probably took hard work. However you're showing up today, at the end of your journaling, pause to check in with yourself. How are you?

After checking in, ask yourself what you need. Start with what you need today. If you need to take an hour to sit and read a book, do it. If you've been thinking about someone who played an important role in your life, reach out. If you need accountability to complete a task you've been putting off, ask someone.

Next, think about what you need for the coming season. Have fun with this! If you need some inspiration, check out the Appendix for ways that I've responded to needs that surfaced in my life. Let your imagination wander and get creative. How would you build in the support you need to continue this journey with joy and peace?

In Closing

Even if we haven't met, we share a kinship that's hard for many to understand. You've heard a bit of my story and been able to share your story on these pages. Pay attention to the stories and questions that moved you. If responding to a certain prompt brought more memories and questions to mind, follow that thread. There were so many topics we didn't get to cover like how disability affects romantic relationships and co-parenting, educational placement, and guardianship or supported decision making. There's additional space to process on the next few pages. Make use of that space to continue the conversation on topics we didn't get a chance to discuss.

My personal mission is to increase belonging for people affected by disability, including caregivers. This book is one way that I am doing that. My hope is that you feel less alone, knowing we hold in common so many of life's unique joys and challenges. Some other ways I've been increasing belonging for people affected by disability is by hosting periodic Caregiver Support Groups, writing about disability advocacy, and serving on my local Board of Education and the Wiedemann-Steiner Syndrome Foundation. By writing, I share the insights I'm gaining through these endeavors. My intention is to equip all of us with skills and tools to navigate life with disability in the world as it presently exists.

If you'd like to learn more, visit www.sarahmspear.com.

Additional Space to Process

Appendix: Ideas for Tending to Ourselves

When my journey has been rough, these tools helped me push on, holding fast to hope. If you're looking for ideas to spark your imagination, here's what sustained me through tough times. I don't practice everything all at once but pick and choose what's needed for a season.

If you're like me, we have a tendency to look at a list like this and feel overwhelmed. We might start feeling like there are so many things we are NOT doing. Instead of going down that path, if you're feeling like you want to tend to yourself in some way but aren't sure where to begin, pick one thing below and try it on for a week or two. If it's helpful, continue. If it's unhelpful or extraordinarily hard, try something else. The ones that stick will benefit you and fit into your life with relative ease.

Spiritual

- Prayer:
  - *Face to Face* by Kenneth Boa, *Celtic Daily Prayer* from the Northumbria Community, and *The Book of Common Prayer*
  - The Lectio365 app for morning and evening reflective prayers
  - Goldenwood's Trellis program for guided listening prayer
- Bible Study:
  - Bible Study Fellowship offers in-person and virtual groups that meet from September to May
  - Inductive Bible Study is an approach that involves observing, interpreting, and applying a passage of scripture
- Writing down one thing, each day, that brought you joy
- Spiritual Direction involves meeting with a Spiritual Director and laying out areas that you would like discernment about. The Spiritual Director listens, reflects back anything they sense God sharing with them, and may encourage listening together for what God is saying.
- Church and local faith communities are great places for encouragement, accountability, and spiritual growth
- Volunteering lets us join God at work

Physical

- Movement everyday, including:
  - Swimming
  - Ballet
  - Walking

- Weight lifting
- Pilates
- Running around with the kids

- Sleep: figure out how many hours you need and reward yourself when you get it
- Food impacts our mental so when you need a re-set, consider starting here
- Water with minimal alcohol and caffeine can also be a helpful re-set
- Vitamins and supplements can improve how we feel. Since every body is unique, ask your doctor to order blood work to determine what you specifically need.

Planning

- Short-term: On Friday afternoons, plan for the week ahead by creating lists of *realistic* tasks for the next week in two categories: personal and professional.
- Long-term: At the beginning of each year, consider setting annual goals across three categories: Vocational, Personal, and Spiritual. At the beginning of each month, set short-term goals based on these annual goals and check in mid-month to see how it's going. Even if goals change, there's value in sitting down to consider where you're headed and how you'll get there.
- Family Scheduling: Whether it's a paper calendar or a Google calendar, writing down your family's agenda can help avoid conflicts. If the calendar is in a place where the kids can see it, they might like checking to see what's coming up. If you co-parent, check in on the weekend about what's coming up and figure out any plans that need to be nailed down.

Mental Health

- Sauna, especially as a mood boost during the dark winter months
- Therapy: Both individual and group therapy are available, depending on what you're working through. Seek a professional who has experience working with others in your situation. This increases the likelihood that your therapist can help you address what's going on. You're in the driver's seat of your therapy; communicate your desires and expectations to your therapist. Good therapists will appreciate this.
- Sunlight exposure helps regulate our circadian rhythms which also impact our moods

About the Author

From disability advocacy in the US to a first ascent in the Himalayas, Sarah Spear's multi-disciplinary life spans the globe. Professionally, Sarah has worked to end human trafficking in the US and abroad, has leveraged entrepreneurship for economic development in the Midwest, and has stopped counterfeit medicine sales in India. Personally, she's caregiver to a daughter who lives with a disability, a military spouse, a surviving sibling, and beloved by God. Sarah loves ballet, backpacking, and cross-country skiing. She lives in Connecticut with her husband and two children. Learn more about Sarah at sarahmspear.com.

If you would like to stay in touch, sign up for Sarah's newsletter by going here: